Countries of the World

Tanzania

by Patricia J. Murphy

Consultant:
Atieno Adala
Outreach Coordinator
African Studies Program
Indiana University

Bridgestone Books
an imprint of Capstone Press
Mankato, Minnesota

Bridgestone Books are published by Capstone Press
151 Good Counsel Drive, P.O. Box 669, Mankato, Minnesota 56002
http://www.capstone-press.com

Library of Congress Cataloging-in-Publication Data
Murphy, Patricia J., 1963–
    Tanzania / by Patricia J. Murphy.
    p. cm.—(Countries of the world)
    Summary: Describes the geography, people, social life and customs, education, basic facts,
animals, and sports of the East African country of Tanzania. Includes a list of words in
Kiswahili and instructions for playing the game of mancala.
    Includes bibliographical references and index.
    ISBN 0-7368-1373-X (hardcover)
    1. Tanzania—Juvenile literature. [1. Tanzania.] I. Title. II. Countries of the world
(Mankato, Minn.)
    DT438 .M87 2003
    967.8—dc21   2001008225

Editorial Credits

Tom Adamson, editor; Karen Risch, product planning editor; Patrick D. Dentinger,
    book designer and illustrator; Alta Schaffer, photo researcher

Photo Credits

Ann & Rob Simpson, 6, 10, 14
AP Photo/George Mwangi, 20
Courtesy of Gayle Zonnefeld, 5 (bottom)
Jason Laurè, cover
Khalfan Mohammad, 8, 12
Michele Burgess, 16
StockHaus Limited, 5 (top)
TRIP/F. Good, 18

1 2 3 4 5 6 07 06 05 04 03 02

Table of Contents

Fast Facts

Name: United Republic of Tanzania
Capital: Dar es Salaam
Population: More than 36 million
Languages: Kiswahili, English, and local languages
Religions: Christian, Muslim, and traditional African religions

Size: 364,900 square miles (945,091 kilometers)
Tanzania is more than twice the size of the U.S. state of California.
Crops: Sisal, cotton, coffee, tea, tobacco, corn, and cloves

Maps

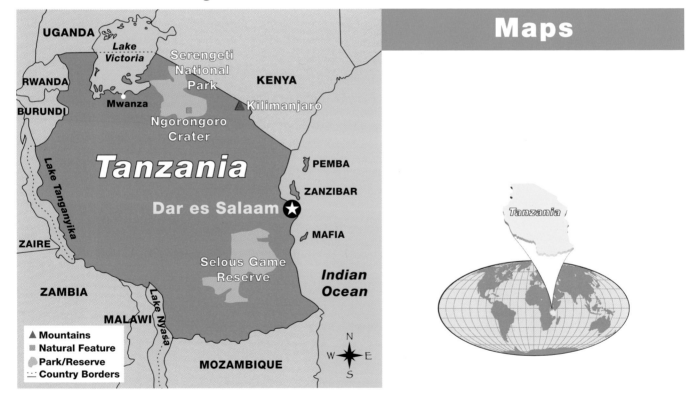

UGANDA
Lake Victoria
Serengeti National Park
RWANDA
KENYA
Mwanza
Kilimanjaro
BURUNDI
Ngorongoro Crater
Tanzania
PEMBA
ZANZIBAR
Lake Tanganyika
Dar es Salaam ★
MAFIA
ZAIRE
Selous Game Reserve
Indian Ocean
ZAMBIA
Lake Nyasa
MALAWI
▲ Mountains
■ Natural Feature
● Park/Reserve
∷ Country Borders
MOZAMBIQUE
N W E S

Tanzania

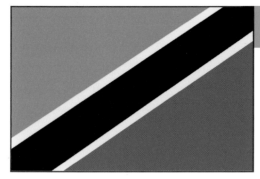

Flag

Tanzania's flag has a blue triangle and a green triangle. One black stripe and two yellow diagonal stripes separate the triangles. Tanzania's flag is a combination of Tanganyika's and Zanzibar's flags. In 1964, these two states combined to form one country. The green and black colors are from Tanganyika's flag. The blue color comes from Zanzibar's flag.

Currency

The unit of currency in Tanzania is the shilling. There are 100 cents in 1 shilling.

In the early 2000s, about 970 shillings equaled 1 U.S. dollar. About 610 shillings equaled 1 Canadian dollar.

The Land

Tanzania is in East Africa. Tanzania's mainland is called Tanganyika. Tanzania also includes the islands Zanzibar, Pemba, and Mafia. These islands lie in the Indian Ocean.

Most of Tanzania's land is a high plateau. Tanzania's highest point is Mount Kilimanjaro, Africa's tallest mountain. It is 19,340 feet (5,895 meters) above sea level.

The Great Rift Valley cuts through Tanzania. This group of fault lines runs through eastern Africa. Two deep lakes are in this valley. They are Lake Tanganyika and Lake Nyasa.

Tanzania lies just south of the equator. This imaginary line circles the middle of Earth. Weather near the equator is hot year-round. Tanzania's coast is hot and steamy. The central plains are hot and dry. Tanzania's highlands are warm.

Snow covers the top of Mount Kilimanjaro year-round.

Life at Home

More than 120 different groups of people live in Tanzania. Each group has its own language and way of life. The largest group is the Sukuma. They live around the city of Mwanza. They raise cattle and grow rice, corn, and cotton.

Many of Tanzania's groups are like the Sukuma. They live in villages. Each village has several compounds. A compound is a group of three or four huts. Most huts are made with wood and mud. These huts have thatched roofs. Some people have homes made of brick and stone with tin roofs.

The Maasai are a small nomadic group. Nomads travel from place to place. They do not have a settled home. The Maasai do not want to change their traditional ways.

Today, many Tanzanians are moving to cities. They may live in apartment buildings. They work in business, service, or government jobs.

Many Tanzanians are moving to cities, like this one on the island of Zanzibar.

Going to School

Tanzanian children begin school at age 7. About two-thirds of Tanzanian children attend primary school. They attend primary school for seven years. Students learn in their native language, Kiswahili.

Most children attend village schools. These schools are free. But some villages are too poor to have schools. They cannot afford to buy books or to pay teachers. Children in these villages learn from their older family members. Other children attend schools where they pay fees and wear uniforms.

One-tenth of Tanzanian children attend secondary school. Students must pass a test to enter this school. They learn English as a second language. Some students go on to college. Others enter training, business, or teaching programs. People who do not attend secondary school find work in the city. Some people work on family farms.

Tanzanian children go to primary school for seven years.

Tanzanian Food

Tanzanians begin meals by washing their hands. They make and eat most of their meals with their hands.

Ugali (oo-GAH-lee) is the most important food in Tanzanians' diets. Ugali is a thick mixture of corn and water. It is made by pounding corn into a flour. The flour is mixed and boiled in water. People eat ugali with green vegetables or in stew.

Tanzanians do not eat meat often. Meat usually is served only for holidays and celebrations. The Maasai drink cow's blood with milk. They only eat meat during certain celebrations. Tanzanians also eat ndizi (n-DEE-zee). Ndizi is a meal of green bananas cooked with meat.

Tanzanians who live near water eat fish such as dagaa (da-GAH) and perch. Much of Tanzania's fish comes from Lakes Victoria, Tanganyika, and Nyasa. Tanzanians catch lobster, crab, and clams from the Indian Ocean.

This market in Zanzibar sells green bananas, which are used in ndizi.

Clothing

Many Tanzanians wear clothes like those found in North America. These clothes include T-shirts, pants, and suits. Other Tanzanians wear traditional or Muslim clothing.

Traditional clothing in Tanzania includes kangas (KAN-gas) and kikois (KI-kois). Women wear kangas. These wraps are worn as skirts, scarves, or shawls. Men wear wraps called kikois.

Muslim women wear black dresses with hoods. The dresses are called bui-buis. Bui-buis cover their head and most of their face. Muslim men wear long white robes called kanzus (KAN-zus). They wear small hats called kofias (KO-fee-uhs).

The Maasai wear bright red wraps. These wraps look like blankets. Maasai are known for their colorful makeup and beaded jewelry. Many Maasai wear neckbands, rings, and headbands.

Many Maasai wear bright red wraps.

Animals

Millions of animals roam the plains, plateaus, and dry lands of Tanzania. Many animals live in Tanzania's national parks and wildlife reserves. Animals roam free on reserves. It is illegal to hunt animals on reserves.

More than 25,000 animals live in Ngorongoro Crater. This bowl-shaped area of land was created long ago when a volcano collapsed. The crater is about 11 miles (18 kilometers) across. Many lions, rhinos, wildebeest, and zebras live in Ngorongoro Crater.

Seregenti National Park also is known for its many types of wildlife. Many of the animals take part in large migrations. Wildebeest and zebras roam freely in the park to find food.

The Selous Game Reserve is the largest wildlife reserve in Africa. It has large populations of elephants, cheetahs, giraffes, and hippos.

Zebras and wildebeest live in Ngorongoro Crater.

Music and Games

Tanzanians enjoy music and have many songs and dances. Each village has ngomas (n-GOH-mas). During these celebrations, they listen to music and enjoy traditional African dancing.

Tanzania's national sport is soccer. Many Tanzanians cheer on their national soccer teams. These teams play in the larger towns. In villages, boys play soccer with balls made of rags.

Many Tanzanians play board games such as bao. Bao players use beans or pebbles and game boards with holes. Some players dig holes in sand. The game involves moving pieces from hole to hole and collecting pieces. The player with the most pieces at the end wins the game.

Many parents cannot afford toys for their children. Children make their own toys out of tin, wires, or empty boxes. They also may play hide-and-seek or jump rope.

Bao is a popular game in Tanzania.

Holidays and Celebrations

Tanzanians celebrate many holidays. Some are national holidays. Others are religious holidays.

Most Tanzanians observe national holidays with parades and speeches. Independence Day is December 9. Tanzanians celebrate their freedom from British rule on this day. Independence Day celebrations include parties and fireworks. Union Day is April 26. Tanzania celebrates the union of Tanganyika and Zanzibar on this day.

Christians celebrate Christmas and Easter. They go to church services and family gatherings. Muslims celebrate Ramadan. Adults fast from sunrise to sunset during this month. At the end of Ramadan, they celebrate Eid el-Fitr. Muslims give gifts to family and friends during this three-day holiday.

In Zanzibar, people celebrate the Festival of the Dhow Countries. This festival honors the countries that have influenced Zanzibar. It takes place every summer and includes a film festival, music, and art.

People enjoy music performances during the Festival of the Dhow Countries.

Hands On: Play Mancala

Bao is a popular game in Tanzania. It is a type of mancala game. Mancala games are popular throughout Africa.

What You Need

Empty egg carton
48 marbles, pebbles, or dried beans

2 bowls
2 players

What You Do

1. Place 4 marbles, pebbles, or beans into each cup in the egg carton.
2. Place the bowls on each end of the egg carton. Each player gets one bowl and one row of the carton.
3. Begin by taking all the pieces from one of the cups on your side of the egg carton. Drop pieces one by one into each cup, moving counterclockwise around the egg carton.
4. Pick up all pieces from the last cup you dropped a piece into and continue in the same direction.
5. Drop one piece into your bowl as you go around the carton.
6. If you drop the last piece into an empty cup, your turn is over.
7. If you drop the last piece into your bowl, choose another cup from your side of the carton and continue.
8. The game is over when one player's side runs out of pieces. The other player puts all the pieces that are left in his or her bowl.
9. The player with the most pieces in his or her bowl is the winner.

Learn to Speak Kiswahili

hello	jambo	(JAHM-bo)
good-bye	kwaheri	(kwah-HAY-ree)
yes	naam	(nah-AHM)
no	la	(LAH)
lion	simba	(SEEM-bah)
one	moja	(MOH-jah)
two	mbili	(MBEE-lee)
three	tatu	(TAH-too)
four	nne	(NNAY)
five	tano	(TAH-noh)

Words to Know

Christian (KRISS-chuhn)—a person who follows the religion of Christianity; Christianity is based on the teachings of Jesus.

fault lines (FAWLT LINEZ)—cracks in Earth's surface

migration (mye-GRAY-shuhn)—the regular movement of animals as they search different places for food

Muslim (MUHZ-luhm)—a person who follows the religion of Islam; Islam is based on the teachings of Muhammad.

plateau (pla-TOH)—a raised area of flat land

sea level (SEE LEV-uhl)—the average surface level of the world's oceans

sisal (SYE-zuhl)—a strong fiber made from a plant

thatched (THACHD)—made of straw

Read More

Heale, Jay. *Tanzania.* Cultures of the World. Tarrytown, N.Y.: Marshall Cavendish, 1998.

McQuail, Lisa. *The Masai of Africa.* First Peoples. Minneapolis: Lerner, 2002.

Useful Addresses and Internet Sites

The Embassy of Tanzania
2139 R Street NW
Washington, DC 20008

Tanzania Embassy in Canada
50 Range Road
Ottawa, ON K1N 8J4
Canada

CIA—The World Factbook—Tanzania
http://www.odci.gov/cia/publications/factbook/geos/tz.html
The Living Africa: National Parks—Tanzania
http://library.thinkquest.org/16645/national_parks/tanzania.shtml

Index